ALGORITHMS

LAST MINUTE CODES

FOR
CODING INTERVIEW

LAST MINUTE CODES

This book is for revision of the questions related to data structures and algorithms which mostly get asked in a coding interview, you need to be familiar with the fundamentals of computing and the basics of data structures and algorithms to read this book.

Best of luck !

LAST MINUTE CODES

TABLE OF CONTENTS

LAST MINUTE CODES

1. Selection Sort

```
vector<int> selectionSort(vector<int>& nums) {
        for(int i=0;i<nums.size()-1;i++){
            int minIndex = i;
            for (int j=i+1;j<nums.size();j++){
                if (nums[minIndex]>nums[j])
                    minIndex = j;
            }
            swap(nums[i], nums[minIndex]);
        }
        return nums;
    }
```

TC : Worst: O(n^2), Best: O(n^2)

2. Insertion Sort

```
void insertionSort(vector<int>& nums){
        if(nums.size() == 0 || nums.size() == 1) return;
        for(int i = 1; i < nums.size(); i++){
            int tmp = nums[i];
            int j = i - 1;
            while(j >= 0 && nums[j] > tmp){
                nums[j + 1] = nums[j];
                j--;
            }
            nums[j + 1] = tmp;
        }
    }
```

TC : Worst: O(n^2), Best: O(n)

3. Merge Sort

```
void merge(vector<int>& nums,int l,int r){
        int mid = l+(r-l)/2;
        int arr[r-l+1];
        int i = l,j = mid+1, index=0;
        while(i<=mid && j<=r){
            if(nums[i]<=nums[j]){
                arr[index++] = nums[i++];
            }else{
                arr[index++] = nums[j++];
            }
        }
        while(i<=mid){
            arr[index++] = nums[i++];
        }
        while(j<=r){
            arr[index++] = nums[j++];
        }

        for(int i=0;i<index;i++){
            nums[i+l] = arr[i];
        }
    }

void mergesort(vector<int>& nums,int l,int r){
        if(l>=r){
            return;
        }
        int mid = l+(r-l)/2;
        mergesort(nums,l,mid);
        mergesort(nums,mid+1,r);
        merge(nums,l,r);
    }

TC :  Worst : O(nlogn), Best : O(nlogn)
```

4. Quick Sort

```
int partition(vector<int>& nums,int l,int r){
        int index = l;

/* moves the element less than pivot to left of it, and the element
greater than pivot to right of it. (pivot = nums[r]) */
        for(int i = l;i<r;i++){
            if(nums[i]<nums[r]){
                swap(nums[i],nums[index]);
                index++;
            }
        }

        swap(nums[index],nums[r]);
        return index; // returns the new pivot
    }

    void quick_sort(vector<int>& nums,int l,int r){
        if(l>=r){
            return;
        }
        int pivot = partition(nums,l,r);
        quick_sort(nums,l,pivot-1);
        quick_sort(nums,pivot+1,r);

    }


TC : Worst : O(n^2), Best : O(nlogn)
```

5. Kadane's algorithm (Find subarrray with maximum sum)

```
int maxSubArray(vector<int>& nums) {
        int sum = 0, mx = INT_MIN;

        for(int i=0;i<nums.size();i++){
            sum += nums[i];
            mx = max(sum,mx);
            sum = max(sum,0);
        }

        return mx;
    }
```

Input: [−2,1,−3,4,−1,2,1,−5, 4]
out : 6

maximum sum subarray :
[4, −1, 2, 1]

TC : O(n)

6. Find duplicate in array of N+1 integers. Each integer is in the range [1,N]

```
// using Floyd's Cycle-Finding Algorithm
int findDuplicate(vector<int>& nums) {
        int p1=nums[0],p2=nums[0];
        p1 = nums[p1];
        p2 = nums[nums[p2]];

        while(p1!=p2){
            p1 = nums[p1];
            p2 = nums[nums[p2]];
        }
        p1 = nums[0];

        while(p1!=p2){
            p1 = nums[p1];
            p2 = nums[p2];
        }

        return p1;
    }
```
TC : O(n), n: length(nums)

input : [1, 3, 4, 2, 5, 2]
out : 2

We can reduce this problem to
'detect cycle in linkedlist' (page 13)
- each nums value is address of the
next node.(head: nums[0])
- there are duplicates in num, so
different nodes points to same value

If we are allowed to change the
array, then we can use this
algorithm also.

```
int solve(vector<int>& nums) {
    for(int i = 0; i < nums.size(); i++) {
        int index = abs(nums[i]) - 1;
        nums[index] *= -1;
        if(nums[index] > 0)
            return abs(nums[i]);
    }
    return -1;
}
```
- nums is also begin used as map
- nums[i] < 0 means it is visited
- nums[i] > 0 after multiplying -1
means it is visited twice!

7. Sort an array containing 0,1 and 2 as elements. (in single pass)

```
void sortArray(vector<int>& nums) {
    int low=0, high = nums.size()-1;
    int mid=0;
    while(mid<=high){
        if(nums[mid]==2){
            swap(nums[high],nums[mid]);
            high--;
        }else if(nums[mid]==0){
            swap(nums[low],nums[mid]);
            low++;
            mid++;
        }else{
            mid++;
        }
    }
}
```

input : [1, 0, 2, 1, 0, 1]

out : [0, 0, 1, 1, 1, 2]

We can just count the number of 0s, 1s and 2s, and then fill the array with 0s first, then 1s and then 2s.
But to do it in single pass, we have to implement the given algorithm using 3 pointers.

TC : O(n), n: length(nums)

8. Merge Intervals : Given an array of intervals, merge the overlapping ones.

```
// intervals[i] = [starti, endi]
vector<vector<int>> merge(vector<vector<int>>& intervals) {
    sort(intervals.begin(),intervals.end());
    if(intervals.size()==0){
        return {};
    }
    vector<int> curr = intervals[0];
    vector<vector<int>> res;
    for(int i=0;i<intervals.size();i++){
        if(curr[1] >= intervals[i][0]){
            curr[1] = max(curr[1],intervals[i][1]);
        }else{
            res.push_back(curr);
            curr = intervals[i];
        }
    }
    res.push_back(curr);
    return res;
}
```

Input: [[1,4],[4,5],[6,7]]

out: [[1,5], [6,7]]

TC : O(n), n: length(intervals)

9. Find next permutation of a number

```
void nextPermutation(vector<int>& nums) { // nums: array of digits
        if(nums.size()<=1){ return;}
        int p1=-1,N=nums.size();
        for(int i=N-2;i>=0;i--){
                if(nums[i]<nums[i+1]){
                        p1 = i;
                        break;
                }
        }
        if(p1!=-1){
                for(int i=N-1;i>=0;i--){
                        if(nums[i]>nums[p1]){
                                swap(nums[i],nums[p1]);
                                break;
                        }
                }
        }
        reverse(nums.begin()+p1+1,nums.end());
}
TC : O(n), n: length(nums)
```

Find 1st decreasing num from right
1 4 7 5 8 7 6 3 2
↑ ← ←
Find num just larger then 5
1 4 7 5 8 7 6 3 2
→ ↑
Swap 5 & 6
1 4 7 6 8 7 5 3 2
Reverse the underlined nums
1 4 7 6 2 3 5 7 8

10. Find Majority Element (Boyer-Moore Voting Algorithm) : Find element which occurs >= N/2 times.

```
int majorityElement(vector<int>& nums) {
        int candidate = nums[0];
        int count = 0;
        for(int i=0;i<nums.size();i++){
                if(count==0){
                        candidate = nums[i];
                }
                if(nums[i]==candidate){
                        count++;
                }else{
                        count--;
                }
        }
        return candidate;
}
TC : O(n), n: length(nums)
```

Input : [1,2,3,2,8,2,2]
out: 2

Other things we can do:
- sort the array and get the middle element.
- randomly pick an index and check if it occurs >=N/2
- use hashmap to store counts and get the required element.

11. Reverse the given String

```
void reverseString(vector<char>& s) {
    for(int i=0;i<s.size()/2;i++) {
        swap(s[i],s[s.size()-1-i]);
    }
}
```
TC : O(n) , n: length(s)

12. Convert Integer to Roman

```
string intToRoman(int num) {
    string arr[] = {"M","CM","D","CD","C","XC","L","XL","X","IX","V","IV","I"};
    int values[] = {1000,900,500,400,100,90,50,40,10,9,5,4,1};
    string roman = "";
    int i=0;
    while(num){
        if(num>=values[i]){
            roman+=arr[i];
            num-=values[i];
        }else{
            i++;
        }
    }
    return roman;
}
```
TC : O(number of digits in num)

13. Convert Roman to Integer

```
int romanToInt(string s) {
    unordered_map<char,int> m = {
        {'I',1},
        {'V',5},
        {'X',10},
        {'L',50},
        {'C',100},
        {'D',500},
        {'M',1000} };
    int sum = m[s.back()];
    for(int i=s.size()-2;i>=0;i--){
        if(m[s[i]] < m[s[i+1]]){
            sum -= m[s[i]];
        }else{
            sum += m[s[i]];
        }
    }
    return sum;
}
```
TC : O(n), n: length(s)

14. Longest Palindromic Substring

```
string longestPalindrome(string s) {
    if(s.size()==0) return "";
    int mx = 1, start = 0;
    for(int i=0;i<s.size();i++){
        int l = i, r = i+1;
        while(l>=0 && r<s.size()){
            if(s[l]!=s[r]){ break; }
            if(r-l+1 > mx){
                mx = r-l+1;
                start = l;
            }
            l--,r++;
        }
        l=i,r=i;
        while(l>=0 && r<s.size()){
            if(s[l]!=s[r]){ break; }
            if(r-l+1 > mx){
                mx = r-l+1;
                start = l;
            }
            l--,r++;
        }
    }
    string ans = s.substr(start,mx);
    return ans;
}
```

Input : "abcdedceze"

out: "cdedc"

TC : O(n^2) , n: length(s)

15. Longest Common Prefix

```
string longestCommonPrefix(vector<string>& strs) {
    if(strs.empty())
        return "";
    string ans="";
    for(int i=0;i<strs[0].size();i++) {
        for(int j=1;j<strs.size();j++) {
            if(i>=strs[j].size() ||  strs[j][i]!=strs[0][i]) {
                return ans;
            }
        }
        ans+=strs[0][i];
    }
    return ans;
}
```

Input: ["apple","ape","april"]
out : "ap"

TC : O(n*m) , n: length(strs), m: minimum length of string

16. Rabin-karp algorithm (Pattern searching)

```
// search pattern pat in string s
int rabinKarpSearch(string& pat, string& s) {
    int q = 101 // a prime number, for use in hashing
    int i, j, pat_hash = 0, s_hash = 0, h = 1, d = 256;

    // h  = pow(d, pat.size()-1)%q
    for(i = 0; i < pat.size()-1; i++) {
        h = (h * d) % q;
    }
    for(i = 0; i < pat.size(); i++) {
        pat_hash = (d * pat_hash + pat[i]) % q;
        s_hash = (d * s_hash + txt[i]) % q;
    }

    for(i = 0; i<=s.size()-pat.size(); i++) {

        if(pat_hash == s_hash) {
            for (j = 0; j < pat.size(); j++) {
                if (s[i+j] != pat[j])
                    break;
            }
            if (j == pat.size())
                return i; // patter found at index i
        }

        if ( i < s.size()-pat.size() ) {
            s_hash = (d*(s_hash - s[i]*h) + s[i+pat.size()])%q;
            if (s_hash < 0)
                s_hash = (s_hash + q);
        }
    }

    return -1;
}
TC : Best case : O(n+m), Worst case : O(n*m)
n : length(s), m : length(pattern)
```

17. KMP algorithm (Pattern searching)

```cpp
// search pattern pat in string s
void KMP(string pat, string s) {
    int m = s.length(), n = pat.length();
    if (n == 0) { return 0; }
    if (m < n) { return -1; }

    // next[i] stores the index of the next best partial match
    int next[n + 1];

    for (int i = 0; i < n + 1; i++) {
        next[i] = 0;
    }

    for (int i = 1; i < n; i++) {
        int j = next[i + 1];
        while (j > 0 && pat[j] != pat[i]) {
            j = next[j];
        }
        if (j > 0 || pat[j] == pat[i]) {
            next[i + 1] = j + 1;
        }
    }

    for (int i = 0, j = 0; i < m; i++) {
        if (s[i] == pat[j]) {
            if (++j == n) {
                cout<<"The pattern found at index "<<i-j+1<<endl;
            }
        }
        else if (j > 0) {
            j = next[j];
            i--;      // i will be incremented in next iteration
        }
    }
}
```

TC: Best case: O(n), Worst case: O(n)
n: length(s)

18. Reverse a Linkedlist

```
Node* reverseList(Node* head) {
        Node* curr = head, *prev = NULL;
        while(curr){
            Node* _next = curr->next;
            curr->next = prev;
            prev = curr;
            curr = _next;
        }
        return prev;
    }
TC : O(n), n: length(head)
```

19. Merge two sorted Linkedlists

```
Node* mergeTwoLists(Node* l1, Node* l2) {
        Node* head = new Node(0);
        Node* curr = head, *temp1 = l1, *temp2 = l2;

        while(temp1 && temp2){
            if(temp1->val < temp2->val){
                curr->next = temp1;
                temp1= temp1->next;
            }else{
                curr->next = temp2;
                temp2=temp2->next;
            }
            curr = curr->next;
        }
        while(temp1){
            curr->next = temp1;
            curr = curr->next;
            temp1=temp1->next;
        }
        while(temp2){
            curr->next = temp2;
            curr = curr->next;
            temp2 = temp2->next;
        }
        return head->next;
    }
TC : O(n + m), n: length(l1), m:length(l2)
```

> Same algorithm can also used to merge sorted arrays, like in merge sort.

20. Find Middle of the Linkedlist

```
Node* middleNode(Node* head) {
        Node* first = head,*second = head;
        while(second && second->next){
            first = first->next;
            second = second->next->next;
        }
        return first;
    }
```

> Second pointer is moving twice the speed of first pointer so,
> When second pointer is at the end, first pointer will be at middle.

TC : O(n), n: length(head)

21. Palindrome LinkedList : check if given linkedlist is palindrome

```
bool isPalindrome(Node* head) {
        Node* mid = middleNode(head);   // implemented.
        Node* right = mid;
        right = reverseList(mid);   // implemented.
        Node* left = head;
        while(left && right){
            if(left->val != right->val){
                return false;
            }
            left = left->next;
            right = right->next;
        }
        return true;
    }
```

TC : O(n), n: length(head)

22. Delete the given Node in the Linkedlist (only the node to be deleted is given)

```
void deleteNode(Node* node) {
        Node* temp = node->next;
        *node = *(node->next);
        delete temp;
    }
```

TC : O(1)

23. Detect Cycle in the Linkedlist, return start point of the cycle.

(Floyd's Cycle-Finding Algorithm)

```
Node* detectCycle(Node *head) {
    if(!head) {
        return NULL;
    }


    Node* p1 = head, *p2 = head;
    p1 = p1->next;

    if(p2->next){
        p2 = p2->next->next;
    }

    while(p1 != p2){
        if(!p2 || !p2->next){
            return NULL;
        }
        p1 = p1->next;
        p2 = p2->next->next;
    }
    // finding start of cycle
    p1 = head;
    while(p1!=p2){
        p1 = p1->next;
        p2 = p2->next;
    }
    return p1;
}
```

p2 is moving moving faster than p1.
So if there is a cycle, then p1 and p2 will meet at some point.

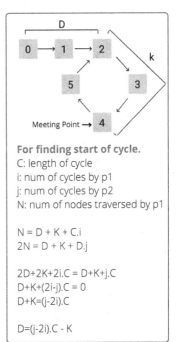

For finding start of cycle.
C: length of cycle
i: num of cycles by p1
j: num of cycles by p2
N: num of nodes traversed by p1

$N = D + K + C.i$
$2N = D + K + D.j$

$2D + 2K + 2i.C = D + K + j.C$
$D + K + (2i-j).C = 0$
$D + K = (j-2i).C$

$D = (j-2i).C - K$

TC : O(n), n: length(head)

24. Implement stack using queue

```cpp
class Stack {
    queue<int> q1, q2;
    int curr_size;
public:
    Stack(){
        curr_size = 0;
    }
    void push(int x){
        curr_size++;
        q2.push(x);
        while (!q1.empty()) {
            q2.push(q1.front());
            q1.pop();
        }
        queue<int> q = q1;
        q1 = q2;
        q2 = q;
    }
    void pop(){
        if (q1.empty())
            return;
        q1.pop();
        curr_size--;
    }
    int top(){
        if (q1.empty())
            return -1;
        return q1.front();
    }
    int size(){
        return curr_size;
    }
};
```

25. Implement queue using stack

```cpp
class Queue {
    stack<int> s1, s2;
public:
    void enQueue(int x) {
        while (!s1.empty()) {
            s2.push(s1.top());
            s1.pop();
        }
        s1.push(x);
        while (!s2.empty()) {
            s1.push(s2.top());
            s2.pop();
        }
    }
    int deQueue() {
        if (s1.empty()) {
            cout << "Q is Empty";
            exit(0);
        }
        int x = s1.top();
        s1.pop();
        return x;
    }

    int top(){
        if (s1.empty()) {
            cout << "Q is Empty";
            exit(0);
        }
        return s1.top();
    }
};
```

26. Find the Next Greater Element for every element of the array.
The Next greater Element for an element x is the first greater element on the right side of x in the array (return -1 if there is no next greater element for x)

```cpp
vector<int> nextGreaterElement(vector<int> arr) {
    vector<int> ans;
    stack<int> s;
    int N = arr.size();
    for(int i=N-1;i>=0;i--) {
        if(s.empty()) {
            ans.push_back(-1);
        }
        else {
            while(!s.empty()) {
                if(s.top()>arr[i]) {
                    ans.push_back(s.top());
                    break;
                }
                else {
                    s.pop();
                }
            }
            if(s.empty()) {
                ans.push_back(-1);
            }
        }
        s.push(arr[i]);
    }
    reverse(ans.begin(),ans.end());
    return ans;
}
```

```
input : [3, 1, 8, 2, 6, 7]
out   : [8, 8, -1, 6, 7, -1]
```

TC: O(n)
n: length(arr)

27. Implement Min Stack

```cpp
class MinStack {
    stack<int> s;
    stack<int> ss; // stores current minimum
public:
    MinStack() {
        s = stack<int>();
        ss = stack<int>();
    }

    void push(int x) {
        s.push(x);
        if(ss.empty()) {
            ss.push(x);
        }
        else {
            if(x<=ss.top()) {
                ss.push(x);
            }
        }
    }

    void pop() {
        if(s.top()==ss.top()) {
            ss.pop();
        }
        s.pop();
    }

    int top() {
        return s.top();
    }

    int getMin() {
        return ss.top();
    }
};
```

28. Check valid parenthesis

Input s contains just the characters '(', ')', '{', '}', '[' and ']'

```
bool isopen(char c) {
    if(c=='{'||c=='('||c=='[')
        return true;
    else
        return false;
}


bool matches(char o,char c) {
    if((o=='['&&c==']' )||(o=='{'&&c=='}') ||(o=='('&&c==')') )
        return true;
    else
        return false;
}


bool isValid(string s) {
    stack<char> st;
    for(int i=0;i<s.size();i++) {
        if(isopen(s[i])) {
            st.push(s[i]);
        }
        else {
            if(st.empty())
                return false;
            if(matches(st.top(),s[i]))
                st.pop();
            else
                return false;
        }
    }
    if(st.empty())
        return true;
    else
        return false;
}
TC: O(n)
n: length(s)
```

input : "{}[[()]]"
out   : true

input : "[()]{}"
out   : false

29. Find the Kth largest element in the array.

```
int findKthLargest(vector<int>& nums, int K) {
    priority_queue<int, vector<int>, greater<int>> pq; // min heap
    for (int num : nums) {
        pq.push(num);
        if (pq.size() > K) {
            pq.pop();
        }
    }
    return pq.top();
}
```

```
nums: [2, 1, 4, 7, 3]
K   : 2

output : 4
```

```
TC: O(n),  space complexity: O(K)
n: length(nums)
```

30. Sort a K sorted array (each element is at most k away from its target position)

```
void sortKSorted(vector<int>& nums, int K){
    int N = arr.size();
    priority_queue<int,vector<int>,greater<int>> p; // min heap

    int r=0; // index upto which elems are in p
    for(r=0;r<=K;r++){
        p.push(nums[r]);
    }

    int i=0; // index upto which array is sorted
    while(r<N){
        nums[i] = p.top();
        p.pop();
        p.push(nums[r]);
        i++;
        r++;
    }
    while(i<N){
        nums[i] = p.top();
        p.pop();
        i++;
    }
}
TC: O(n)
n: length(nums)
```

```
nums: [2, 6, 3, 12, 36, 9]
K : 3

out : [2, 3, 6, 9, 12, 36]
```

31. Two sum : find a pair in array whose sum equals to the target.

```cpp
vector<int> twoSum(vector<int>& nums, int target) {
        unordered_map<int,int> m;  // hashmap
        for(int i=0;i<nums.size();i++){
            m[nums[i]] = i;
        }
        for(int i=0;i<nums.size();i++){
            if(m.find(target-nums[i])!=m.end() && m[target-nums[i]]!=i){
                return {i,m[target-nums[i]]};
            }
        }
        return {};
    }
```

input : [10,4,1,3,2] , 7
out   : [4,3]

TC : O(n), n: length(nums)

32. Longest Consecutive Sequence : find length of longest consecutive sequence from given array.

```cpp
int longestConsecutive(vector<int>& nums) {
        unordered_set<int> st;   // hash set
        for(int a : nums){
            st.insert(a);
        }
        int count = 0;
        int mx = 0;
        for(int a : nums){
            if(st.count(a-1)==0){
                count = 1;
                int x = a+1;
                while(st.count(x)){
                    count++;
                    x++;
                }
                mx = max(count,mx);
            }
        }
        return mx;
    }
```

input : [10, 4, 20, 1, 3, 2]
out   : 4

longest consecutive
sequence is 1,2,3,4

TC : O(n), length(nums)

33. Copy Linkedlist with random pointer.

```
Node* copyRandomLinkedlist(Node* head) {
        unordered_map<Node*,Node*> m;   // hashmap
        Node* temp = head;
        while(temp){
            m[temp] = new Node(temp->val);
            temp = temp->next;
        }
        temp = head;
        while(temp){
            m[temp]->next = m[temp->next];
            m[temp]->random = m[temp->random];
            temp = temp->next;
        }
        return m[head];
    }
TC : O(n), n : length(head)
```

```
class Node{
    int val;
    Node* next;
    Node* random;
}
```

34. Find Longest Substring without repeating characters.

```
int lengthOfLongestSubstring(string s) {
        unordered_set<int> st;   // hash set
        int mx = 0, l=0, r=0;
        while(r < s.size()){
            if(st.count(s[r])){
                while(s[l]!=s[r]){
                    st.erase(s[l]);
                    l++;
                }
                l++;
            }else{
                st.insert(s[r]);
            }
            mx = max(r-l+1,mx);
            r++;
        }
        return mx;
    }
TC : O(n), n: length(s)
```

```
input : "abbdcabc"
out   : 4

answer is "bdca"
```

35. Implement LRU Cache

We can use Hashmap and Doubly Linkedlist.
Hashmap will be used to access any node of linkedlist in O(1) time.
We can remove or add the given node in linkedlist in O(1) time.
Every interacted element will be moved at start of the linkedlist, so the least recently used ones will be at the end of the linkedlist.
When maximum capacity is reached, tail of the linkedlist will be removed.

```cpp
class LRU_Cache {

    Doubly_linkedlist list; // implement a doubly linkedlist
    unordered_map<int,Node*> m; // hashmap
    int max_size;

    public :
    LRU_Cache( int _max_size) {
        this->max_size = _max_size
    }

    int get (int key) {
        Node* node = m[key];
        list.detachNode(node); // detaches the node from the linkedlist
        list.addToHead(node); // add the node to the start
        return node.value
    }
    // TC: O(1)

    void set ( int key, int value) {
        if (m.size() == max_size) {
            Node* nodeToRemove = list.getTail();
            list.removeTail(); // removes the tail node from linkedlist
            int keyToRemove = nodeToRemove.key;
            m.erase(key); // removed the element from hashmap
        }

        Node* node = new Node(key,value);
        list.addToHead(node);
        m[key] = node;
    }
    // TC: O(1)
}
```

36. Two sum : find a pair whose sum equals to the target.

```
bool twoPointers(vector<int> a, int target) {
    sort(a.begin(),a.end());
    int i = 0;int j = a.length - 1;
    while (i < j) {
        int sum = a[i] + a[j];
        if (sum == k) {return true;}
        else if (sum < k) {
            i++;
        } else {
            j--;
        }
    }
    return false;
}
TC : O(nlogn) , (O(n) if array is already sorted), n: length(a)
```

input : [10,4,1,3,2] , 7
out   : true

pair : [4,3]

37. Three Sum : find triplets whose sum equals to the target

```
vector<vector<int>> threeSum(vector<int>& nums,int target) {
    sort(nums.begin(),nums.end());
    vector<vector<int>> ans;
    for(int i=0;i<nums.size();i++){
        if(i>0 && nums[i] == nums[i-1]){ continue; }
        int l = i+1,r = nums.size()-1;
        while(l<r){
            if(l>i+1 && nums[l]==nums[l-1]){
                l++; continue;
            }
            if(r<nums.size()-1 && nums[r]==nums[r+1]){
                r--; continue;
            }
            int sum = nums[i] + nums[l] + nums[r];
            if(sum == target){
                ans.push_back({nums[i],nums[l],nums[r]});
                l++;
            }else if(sum < target){
                l++;
            }else{
                r--;
            }
        }
    }
    return ans;
}
TC : O(n^2) , n: length(nums)
```

input : [10,4,1,3,2] , 9
out   : [[4,3,2]]

Similar algortithm as done in twosum problem.

38. Trapping Rainwater : Given an array of height of bars (width = 1), calculate the amount of water trapped

```cpp
int trap(vector<int>& height) {
        int N = height.size();
        int left=0, right=N-1, res=0;
        int maxleft=0, maxright=0;
        while(left<=right){
            if(height[left]<=height[right]){
                if(height[left]>=maxleft) {
                    maxleft=height[left];
                }
                else {
                    res+=maxleft-height[left];
                }
                left++;
            }
            else{
                if(height[right]>=maxright) {
                    maxright= height[right];
                }
                else {
                    res+=maxright-height[right];
                }
                right--;
            }
        }
        return res;
 }
TC : O(n) , n: length(height)
```

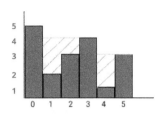

```
input : [5, 2, 3, 4, 1, 3]
out   : 5
```

39. Remove duplicates from sorted array. (return the new length of array)

```cpp
int removeDuplicates(vector<int>& nums) {
        if(nums.empty()) return 0;
        int index=0;
        for(int i=0;i<nums.size();i++) {
            if(nums[i]!=nums[index]) {
                nums[++index] = nums[i];
            }
        }
        return index+1;
    }
TC : O(n), n: length(nums)
```

```
input : [1,1,2,3,3,6,7,7]
out   : 5

nums : [1,2,3,6,7,6,7,7]
```

40. Combination Sum (return list of numbers from given array whose sum = target)

```cpp
vector<vector<int>> res;
void util(vector<int>& nums,vector<int> ans,int target,int i){
        if(target == 0){
            res.push_back(ans);
            return;
        }
        if(i == nums.size())  return;
        util(nums,ans,target,i+1);
        while(target - nums[i]>=0) {
            ans.push_back(nums[i]);
            target-=nums[i];
            util(nums,ans,target,i+1);
        }
    }

vector<vector<int>> combinationSum(vector<int>& nums, int target){
        util(nums,{},target,0);
        return res;
    }
```

TC : O(2^n) , n: length(nums)

41. Print sum of all subsets of given array.

```cpp
void subsetSums(vector<int>& arr, int l, int r, int sum=0) {
    if (l > r){
        cout << sum << " ";
        return;
    }
    subsetSums(arr, l+1, r, sum+arr[l]);
    subsetSums(arr, l+1, r, sum);
}
```

TC : O(2^n), n: length(arr)

42. Generate all pairs of valid parenthesis

```
void solve(string s,int open,int close,int n,vector<string>& res){
    if(open==n && close==n){
        res.push_back(s);
        return;
    }
    if(open<n){
        s.push_back('(');
        solve(s,open+1,close,n,res);
        s.pop_back();
    }
    if(open<=n && open>close){
        s.push_back(')');
        solve(s,open,close+1,n,res);
    }
}
// n : number of parenthesis pairs to generate
vector<string> generateString(int n) {
    vector<string> res;
    solve("",0,0,n,res);
    return res;
}
TC : O(2^n)
```

```
input : 2
out : {
    "()()",
    "(())"
}
```

43. Generate all possible permutations of the given array

```
void util(vector<int> nums,int i,int j,vector<vector<int>>& res) {
    if(i==j) {
        res.push_back(nums);
        return;
    }

    for(int k=i;k<=j;k++) {
        swap(nums[i],nums[k]);
        util(nums,i+1,j);
        swap(nums[i],nums[k]);
    }
}
vector<vector<int>> permute(vector<int>& nums) {
    vector<vector<int>> res;
    util(nums,0,nums.size()-1);
    return res;
}
TC : O(2^n), n: length(nums)
```

44. Place N queens on NxN chess board. (return all combinations)

```cpp
bool isValid(vector<string>& board,int x,int y){
    int n = board.size();
    for(int i = 0;i<board.size();i++){
        if(board[i][y]=='Q' || board[x][i]=='Q') return false;
    }
    int i=x,j=y;
    while(i<n && j<n){
        if(board[i][j]=='Q') return false;
        i++; j++;
    }
    i=x,j=y;
    while(i<n && j>=0){
        if(board[i][j]=='Q') return false;
        i++; j--;
    }
    i=x,j=y;
    while(i>=0 && j<n){
        if(board[i][j]=='Q') return false;
        i--; j++;
    }
    i=x,j=y;
    while(i>=0 && j>=0){
        if(board[i][j]=='Q') return false;
        i--; j--;
    }
    return true;
}
vector<vector<string>> res;
void solve(vector<string> board,int row){
    if(row==board.size()){ res.push_back(board); return; }
    for(int i=0;i<board.size();i++){
        if(isValid(board,row,i)){
            board[row][i]='Q';
            solve(board,row+1);
            board[row][i]='.';
        }
    }
}
vector<vector<string>> solveNQueens(int n) {
    vector<string> v(n,string(n,'.'));
    solve(v,0);
    return res;
} // TC : O(2^n)
```

45. Preorder Traversal

```
// recursive
void preorder(Node* root) {
    if(root == NULL){ return; }
    cout<< root->val <<" ";
    preorder(root->left);
    preorder(root->right);
}


// Iterative
vector<int> preorder(Node* root) {
        if(root==NULL) { return {}; }
        vector<int> preorder;
        stack<pair<Node*,int>> st;
        st.push({root,0});
        while(!st.empty()){
            pair<Node*,int> p = st.top();
            Node* curr = p.first;
            int state = p.second;
            st.pop();
            if(state<2){
                st.push({curr,state+1});
            }
            if(state == 0){
                preorder.push_back(curr->val);
            }else if(state == 1){
                if(curr->left){
                    st.push({curr->left,0});
                }
            }else if(state == 2){
                if(curr->right){
                    st.push({curr->right,0});
                }
            }
        }
        return preorder;
    }
TC : O(n), n: numOfNodes(root)
```

In the recursive algorithm, the node remains in 3 states.
state 0: print the value
state 1: process left node
state 2: process right node

So we can simulate the same procedure in iterative way.
We will store node with its current state in stack, and process it accordingly.

Same for inorder and postorder also.

46. Inorder Traversal

```
// recursive
void inorder(Node* root) {
   if(root == NULL){ return; }
   inorder(root->left);
   cout<< root->val <<" ";
   inorder(root->right);
}


// Iterative
vector<int> inorder(Node* root) {
        if(root==NULL) { return {}; }
        vector<int> inorder;
        stack<pair<Node*,int>> st;
        st.push({root,0});
        while(!st.empty()){
            pair<Node*,int> p = st.top();
            Node* curr = p.first;
            int state = p.second;
            st.pop();
            if(state<2){
                st.push({curr,state+1});
            }
            if(state == 0){
                if(curr->left){
                  st.push({curr->left,0});
                }
            }else if(state == 1){
                inorder.push_back(curr->val);
            }else if(state == 2){
                if(curr->right){
                    st.push({curr->right,0});
                }
            }
        }
        return inorder;
    }
TC : O(n), n: numOfNodes(root)
```

47. Postorder Traversal

```cpp
// recursive
void postorder(Node* root) {
   if(root == NULL){ return;
   postorder(root->left);
   postorder(root->right);
   cout<< root->val <<" ";
}


// Iterative
vector<int> postorder(Node* root) {
        if(root==NULL) { return {}; }
        vector<int> postorder;
        stack<pair<Node*,int>> st;
        st.push({root,0});
        while(!st.empty()){
            pair<Node*,int> p = st.top();
            Node* curr = p.first;
            int state = p.second;
            st.pop();
            if(state<2){
                st.push({curr,state+1});
            }
            if(state == 0){
                if(curr->left){
                   st.push({curr->left,0});
                }
            }else if(state == 1){
                if(curr->right){
                   st.push({curr->right,0});
                }

            }else if(state == 2){
                    postorder.push_back(curr->val);
            }
        }
        return postorder;
    }
TC : O(n), n: numOfNodes(root)
```

48. Height of Binary Tree

```
int height(Node* root) {
    if (root == NULL)
        return 0;
    else {
        int leftHeight = height(root->left);
        int rightHeight = height(root->right);
        return 1+ max(leftHeight, rightHeight);
    }
}
```

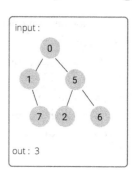

input :

out : 3

TC : O(n), n: numOfNodes(root)

49. Diameter of Binary Tree: The diameter of a binary tree is the length of the longest path between any two nodes in a tree

```
int solve(Node* root,int &res){

    if(root==nullptr){
        return 0;
    }

    int l = solve(root->left,res);
    int r = solve(root->right,res);

    int t = 1 + l + r;

    res = max(res,t);
    return 1+max(l,r);

}
```

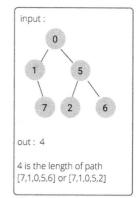

input :

out : 4

4 is the length of path [7,1,0,5,6] or [7,1,0,5,2]

```
int diameterOfBinaryTree(Node* root) {
    int res = 0;
    solve(root,res);

    if(res==0)
        return 0;
    return res-1;
}
```

TC : O(n), n: numOfNodes(root)

50. Convert to Sum Tree : Convert it such that every node's value is equal to sum of its left and right subtree.

```
int convert(Node *root) {
    if(root == NULL)
        return 0;
    int temp = root->val;
    root->val = convert(root->left) + convert(root->right);
    return root->val + temp;
}
```

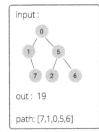

TC : O(n), n: numOfNodes(root)

51. Maximum path sum in Binary Tree

```
int solve(Node* root,int& res){
    if(root == NULL){
        return 0;
    }

    int l = solve(root->left,res);
    int r = solve(root->right,res);

    int temp = max(root->val +  max(l,r),root->val);

    int ans = l + r + root->val;
    res = max({res,ans,temp});
    return temp;
}

int maxPathSum(Node* root) {
    int res = INT_MIN;
    solve(root,res);
    return res;
}
```

TC : O(n), n: numOfNodes(root)

52. Construct Binary Tree from preorder and inorder

```
Node* helper(vector<int>& preorder,int i1,int j1,vector<int>& inorder,int
i2,int j2) {
    if(i1 >= j1 || i2 >= j1)
        return NULL;

    int mid = preorder[i1];
    auto t = find(inorder.begin() + i2,inorder.begin() + j2,mid);
    int dist = t - inorder.begin() - i2;
    Node* root = new Node(mid);
    root->left=helper(preorder,i1+1,i1+1+dist,inorder,i2,i2 + dist);
    root->right=helper(preorder,i1+1+dist,j1,inorder,i2+dist + 1,j2);
    return root;
}


Node* buildTree(vector<int>& preorder, vector<int>& inorder) {
    return helper(preorder,0,preorder.size(),inorder,0,inorder.size());
}
TC : O(n) , n: length(preorder)
```

53. Lowest Common Ancestor in a Binary Tree

```
Node* lowestCommonAncestor(Node* root, Node* p, Node* q) {
    if(root==NULL || root==p || root==q)
        return root;
    Node* left = lowestCommonAncestor(root->left,p,q);
    Node* right = lowestCommonAncestor(root->right,p,q);

    if(left && right) {
        return root;
    }
    if(left && !right) {
        return left;
    }
    if(!left && right) {
        return right;
    }
    return NULL;
}
TC : O(n), n: numOfNodes(root)
```

input :
root:

p: 7, q: 2
out: 0

p:2, q:6
out: 5

GRAPH   33

54. Depth First Search

```
void dfs_util(int u,vector<vector<int>>& adj,vector<int>& visited){
        visited[u] = 1;
        cout<<u<<" ";
        for(auto v : adj[u]){
            if(visited[v] == 0){
                dfs_util(v,adj,visited);
            }
        }
        visited[u] = 2;
}


void dfs(vector<vector<int>>& adj, int src){
    vector<int> visited(adj.size(),0);
    dfs_util(src,adj,visited);
}
TC : O(v+e) , v: numOfVertices(adj), e: numOfEdges(adj)
```

55. Breadth First Search

```
void bfs(vector<vector<int>>& adj,int s) {
    bool *visited = new bool[V];
    for(int i = 0; i < V; i++)
        visited[i] = false;

    queue<int> q;
    visited[s] = true;
    q.push(s);

    while(!q.empty()) {
        s = q.front();
        cout<<s<<" ";
        q.pop();

        for (auto i=adj[s].begin(); i!=adj[s].end(); i++) {
            if (!visited[*i]) {
                visited[*i] = true;
                q.push(*i);
            }
        }
    }
}


TC : O(v+e), v: numOfVertices(adj), numOfEdges(adj)
```

GRAPH 34

56. Dijsktra's Algorithm (Shortest path from source to destination)

```
void dijsktras(vector<vector<pair<int,int>>>& adj, int src,int des){
    int V = adj.size();
    // min heap
    priority_queue<pair<int,int>,vector<pair<int,int>>,greater<pair<int,int>>> pq;
    vector<int> dist(V, INF);
    dist[src] = 0;
    pq.push({0, src});
    while (!pq.empty()) {
        int u = pq.top().second;
        pq.pop();
        for (auto a : adj[u]) {
            int v = a.first;
            int weight = a.second; // edge weight between u and v
              if (dist[v] > dist[u] + weight){ // update dist[v]
                 dist[v] = dist[u] + weight;
                 pq.push({dist[v], v});
              }
         }
     }
    return dist[des];
}
```

adj[u][i]: {connected node, weight}
pq: min heap
dist[i] : distance of i from src

TC : O(elogv), v: numOfVertices(adj), e: numOfEdges(adj)

57. Detect Cycle in a directed graph

```
bool dfs(int u,vector<vector<int>>& adj,int* color) {
    visited[u]=1;
    for(int v : adj[u]) {
        if(visited[v]==1)
            return true;
        else if(visited[v]==0 && dfs(v,adj,visited))
            return true;
    }
    visited[u]=2;
    return false;
}
bool isCyclic(int V, vector<vector<int>>& adj) {
    int* visited = new int[V];
    memset(visited,0,V*sizeof(int));
    for(int i=0;i<V;i++) {
        if(visited[i]==0 && dfs(i,adj,visited))
            return true;
    }
    return false;
}
```

TC : O(v+e), v: numOfVertices(adj), e: numOfEdges(adj)

GRAPH 35

58. Topological sort

```
void dfs(int u, vector<vector<int>>& adj, vector<int>& visited,
vector<int>& order,bool& isPossible){
        if(!isPossible){ return; }
        visited[u] = 1;
        for(auto v : adj[u]){
            if(visited[v]==1){
                isPossible = false;
                return;
            }
            if(visited[v] == 0){
                dfs(v,adj,visited,order,isPossible);
            }
        }
        order.push_back(u);
        visited[u] = 2;
    }


vector<int> topologicalSort(vector<vector<int>>& adj){
        vector<int> order, visited(adj.size());
        bool isPossible = true;
        for(int i = 0;i<adj.size();i++){
            if(visited[i] == 0){
                dfs(i,adj,visited,order,isPossible);
            }
        }
        reverse(order.begin(),order.end());
        if(!isPossible){ return {}; }
        return order;
    }


TC : O(v+e), v: numOfVertices(adj), e: numOfEdges(adj)
```

GRAPH

36

59. Disjoint Set Union (DSU)

```cpp
vector<int> parent, rank;
void make_set(int v) {
    parent[v] = v;
    rank[v] = 0;
}


// find root of the set, also doing path compression
int find_set(int v) {
    if (v == parent[v])
        return v;

    // we are updating the parent[v] before returning
    // (path compression)
    return parent[v] = find_set(parent[v]);
}


// union by rank based on the depth of the trees
void union_sets(int a, int b) {
    a = find_set(a);
    b = find_set(b);
    if (a != b) {
        if (rank[a] < rank[b])
            swap(a, b);
        parent[b] = a;
        if (rank[a] == rank[b])
            rank[a]++;
    }
}
```

joining node with less depth as child of node with more depth

parent[i] stores index of immediate ancestor of i.
rank[i] is the depth of the tree with node i as root.

Optimizations we have done.
- Path compression in **find_set**.
- union by rank based on the depth of the tree in **union_set**.

Due to these optimizations :
TC would be nearly **constant** for all queries.

GRAPH 37

60. Minimum spanning tree (Kruskal's Algorithm)

```
// using Disjoint Set Union
// Disjoint Set Union implementation (done on previous page).
void make_set(int v);
int find_set(int v);
void union_set(int a,int b);


struct Edge {
    int u, v, weight;
    bool operator<(Edge const& other) {
        return weight < other.weight;
    }
};


int n;
vector<Edge> edges; // edges of the given graph


int cost = 0;
vector<Edge> result; // edges of the generated MST
parent.resize(n);
rank.resize(n);
for (int i = 0; i < n; i++)
    make_set(i);


sort(edges.begin(), edges.end());


for (Edge e : edges) {
    if (find_set(e.u) != find_set(e.v)) {
        cost += e.weight;
        result.push_back(e);
        union_sets(e.u, e.v);
    }
}


TC : O(elogv), v: numOfVertices, e: numOfEdges
```

> **Steps** :
> - Sort all the edges of the graph in non-decreasing order of weights.
> - Then put each vertex in its own tree (i.e. it's set) via calls to the **make_set** function - it will take a total of O(N).
> - Iterate through all the edges (in sorted order) and for each edge determine whether the ends belong to different trees (with two **find_set** calls in O(1) each).
> - Finally, we need to perform the union of the two trees (sets), for which the DSU **union_sets** function will be called - also in O(1)

GRAPH

38

61. Minimum spanning tree (Prim's Algorithm)

```cpp
struct Edge {
    int w = INF, to = -1;
    bool operator<(Edge const& other) const {
        return make_pair(w, to) < make_pair(other.w, other.to);
    }
};
int n;
vector<vector<Edge>> adj;   // adjacency list
void prim() {
    int total_weight = 0;
    vector<Edge> min_e(n);   // min_e[i]
    min_e[0].w = 0;
    set<Edge> q; // stores not yet selected vertices
    q.insert({0, 0});
    vector<bool> selected(n, false);
    for (int i = 0; i < n; ++i) {
        if (q.empty()) {
            cout << "No MST!" << endl;
            exit(0);
        }
        int v = q.begin()->to;
        selected[v] = true;
        total_weight += q.begin()->w;
        q.erase(q.begin());
        if (min_e[v].to != -1)
            cout << v << " " << min_e[v].to << endl;
        for (Edge e : adj[v]) {
            if (!selected[e.to] && e.w < min_e[e.to].w) {
                q.erase({min_e[e.to].w, e.to});
                min_e[e.to] = {e.w, v};
                q.insert({e.w, e.to});
            }
        }
    }
    cout << total_weight << endl;
}
TC : O(elogv), v: numOfVertices, e: numOfEdges
```

---

adj: adjacency list
min_e[i]: store the smallest edge from vertex i to already selected vertex.
q: filled with not yet selected vertices in increasing order of weights min_e.

The algorithm does **n** steps, on each of which it selects the vertex **v** with the smallest weight **min_e** (by extracting it from the beginning of the queue), and then looks through all the edges from this vertex and updates the values in **min_e** (during an update we also need to also remove the old edge from the queue **q** and put in the new edge).

GRAPH   39

62. Bipartite check : Check if graph is bipartite

```cpp
bool bfs(int s,vector<vector<int>>& graph,vector<int>& color) {
        queue<int> q;
        q.push(s);
        while(!q.empty()) {
            int u = q.front();
            q.pop();
            int fillcolor;
            if(color[u]==0)
                fillcolor=1;
            else
                fillcolor=0;

            for(int i=0;i<graph[u].size();i++) {
                if(color[graph[u][i]]==color[u]) {
                    return false;
                }
                else {
                    if(color[graph[u][i]]==-1) {
                        color[graph[u][i]]=fillcolor;
                        q.push(graph[u][i]);
                    }
                }
            }
        }
        return true;
}

bool isBipartite(vector<vector<int>>& graph) {
        vector<int> color(graph.size(),-1);
        for(int i=0;i<graph.size();i++) {
            if(color[i]==-1) {
                color[i]=0;
                if(bfs(i,graph,color) == false)
                    return false;
            }
        }
        return true;
}
TC : O(v+e), v: numOfVertices(graph), e: numOfEdges(graph)
```

63. Coin Change : coins array represents coins of different denomination, return the minimum number of coins required to make up the amount.

```
int coinChange(vector<int>& coins, int amount) {
        int n = coins.size();
        int dp[amount+1];
        fill(dp,dp+amount+1,INT_MAX-1);
        dp[0]=0;
        for(int i=1;i<=amount;i++) {
            for(int j=0;j<coins.size();j++) {
                if(coins[j]<=i) {
                    dp[i] = min(dp[i],dp[i-coins[j]]+1);
                }
            }
        }
        if(dp[amount]==INT_MAX-1)
            return -1;
        return dp[amount];
    }
TC : O(amount * n), n: length(coins)
```

```
input :
coins: [1,2,5]
amount: 11

output: 3

(11 = 5 + 5 + 1)
```

64. Longest Increasing Subsequence

```
int LIS(vector<int>& nums) {
        int n = nums.size();
        if(n==0)
            return 0;
        vector<int> lis(n,1);
        for(int i=1;i<n;i++) {
            for(int j=0;j<i;j++) {
                if(nums[i]>nums[j]) {
                    lis[i] = max(1+lis[j],lis[i]);
                }
            }
        }
        return *max_element(lis.begin(),lis.end());
    }
TC : O(n^2), n: length(nums)
```

```
nums: [0,1,0,2,6,5]
output: 4

LIS : [0,1,2,5]
```

65. Longest common subsequence

```
    int dp[1000][1000];
    int solve(string& s1,string& s2,int n,int m){
        if(n==0||m==0){ return 0; }
        if(dp[n][m]!=-1){
            return dp[n][m]; // return cached value
        }
        if(s1[n-1]==s2[m-1]){
            return  dp[n][m] = 1 + solve(s1,s2,n-1,m-1);
        }
        return dp[n][m]= max(solve(s1,s2,n,m-1),solve(s1,s2,n-1,m));
    }
    int longestCommonSubsequence(string s1, string s2) {
        memset(dp,-1,sizeof(dp));
        return solve(s1,s2,s1.size(),s2.size());
    }
TC : O(n*m), n: length(s1), m: length(s2)
```

```
input :
s1: "ABCDGH"
s2: "AEDFHR"
output: 3

LCS: "ADA"
```

66. Subset sum : Find if there is a subset whose sum equals to the given sum.

```
struct hash_pair{
    int operator()(pair<int,int> p) const {
        return p.first ^ p.second;
    }
};
unordered_map<pair<int,int>,int,hash_pair> dp;
bool solve(vector<int>& nums,int n,int s){
    if(s==0){
        return true;
    }
    if(n==nums.size() || s<0){
        return false;
    }
    pair<int,int> key = {n,s};
    if(dp.count(key)) return dp[key];
    bool ans = solve(nums,n+1,s-nums[n]) || solve(nums,n+1,s);
    return dp[key]=ans;
}
bool subsetSum(vector<int>& nums,int sum) {
    return solve(nums,0,sum);
}
TC : O(n*sum), n: length(nums)
```

```
input :
nums: [3,34,4,12,5,2]
sum: 9
output: true

subset: [5,4]
```

67. Edit Distance : Minimum operations required to convert string a to b by inserting / deleting / replacing character

```
int solve(string& a,string& b,int m,int n) {
    int dp[m+1][n+1];
    for(int i=0;i<=m;i++) {
        for(int j=0;j<=n;j++) {
            if(i==0||j==0) {
                dp[i][j]=max(i,j);
            } else if(a[i-1]==b[j-1]) {
                dp[i][j] = dp[i-1][j-1];
            } else {
                dp[i][j] = 1 + min({dp[i-1][j-1],dp[i][j-1],dp[i-1][j]});
            }
        }
    }
    return dp[m][n];
}
```

```
input :
a: "sunday"
b: "saturday"
output: 3

steps:
replace n with r,
insert t,
insert r
```

TC : O(n*m), n: length(a), m: length(b)

68. Matrix chain multiplication : Find the most efficient way to multiply matrices. ith matrix has the dimensions (arr[i-1] x arr[i])

```
int dp[101][101];
int solve(vector<int>& arr,int i,int j){
    if(i>=j) { return 0; }
    if(dp[i][j]!=-1) {
        return dp[i][j];
    }
    int ans=INT_MAX,t;
    for(int k=i;k<=j-1;k++) {
        t = solve(arr,i,k)+solve(arr,k+1,j) + arr[i-1]*arr[k]* arr[j];
        ans = min(t,ans);
    }

    return dp[i][j] = ans;
}
```

```
input: [10, 20, 30, 40, 30]
output: 30000

soln: ((AB)C)D
=> 10*20*30 +
10*30*40 + 10*40*30
```

```
int matrixChainMultiplication(vector<int>& arr){
    memset(dp,-1,sizeof(dp));
    return solve(arr,1,arr.size()-1);
}
```

TC : O(n^3), n: length(arr)

69. Job scheduling : Find maximum profit by sheduling jobs such that no two jobs' time range overlaps.

```
int dp[1000000];
int findNextJob(vector<vector<int>>& v,int i){
    for(int j=i+1;j<v.size();j++){
        if(v[j][0]>=v[i][1]){
            return j;
        }
    }
    return v.size();
}
int solve(vector<vector<int>>& v,int i){
        if(i == v.size()){ return 0; }
        if(dp[i]!=-1){
            return dp[i];
        }
        int ans = 0;
        ans = v[i][2] + solve(v,findNextJob(v,i));
        ans = max(ans,solve(v,i+1));
        return dp[i] = ans;
    }
// jobs[i] = {startTime, endTime, profit};
int jobScheduling(vector<vector<int>>& jobs) {
        sort(jobs.begin(),jobs.end(),[](auto& a,auto& b){
            return a[0] < b[0];
        });
        memset(dp,-1,sizeof(dp));
        return solve(jobs,0);
    }
TC : O(n) , n: length(jobs)
```

jobs : [
  [1, 2, 50],
  [3, 5, 20],
  [6, 19, 100]
  [2, 100, 200]]

output: 250
jobs scheduled:
index 0,3

70. 0 / 1 Knapsack problem : v contains values of items, weight contains weights of items, find maximum total value of items that can be put in bag of capacity W.

```
int solve(vector<int>& v,vector<int>& weight,int W){
    int N = v.size(), dp[W+1];
    memset(dp,0,sizeof(dp));
    for(int i=0;i<N;i++) {
        for(int w=W;w>=weight[i];w--) {
            dp[w]=max(v[i]+dp[w-weight[i]],dp[w]);
        }
    }

    return dp[W];
}
TC : O(n*W), n: length(weight)
```

v: [24, 18, 18, 10]
weight: [24,10,10,7]

output: 36
items selected:
index 1,2

71. Minimum Path sum in a matrix (minimize path from (0,0) to (n,m))

```
int dp[1000][1000];
int solve(vector<vector<int>>& grid,int x,int y){
    if(x == grid.size() || y==grid[0].size()){
        return INT_MAX/2;
    }
    if(x == grid.size()-1 && y==grid[0].size()-1){
        return grid[x][y];
    }
    if(dp[x][y]!=-1){
        return dp[x][y];
    }
    int ans = grid[x][y] + min(solve(grid,x+1,y),solve(grid,x,y+1));
        return dp[x][y] = ans;
    }
    int minPathSum(vector<vector<int>>& grid) {
        memset(dp,-1,sizeof(dp));
        return solve(grid,0,0);
    }
TC : O(n*m), n: grid.size(), m: grid[0].size()
```

grid: [
   [1,3,1],
   [1,5,1],
   [4,2,1]]

output: 7
1 → 3 → 1 → 1 → 1

72. Maximum sum increasing subsequence

```
int maxSumIS(vector<int>& arr){
    int i, j, max = 0, N = arr.size();
    int dp[N];

    for (i = 0; i < N; i++)
        dp[i] = arr[i];

    for (i = 1; i < N; i++) {
        for (j = 0; j < i; j++) {
            if (arr[i] > arr[j] && dp[i] < dp[j] + arr[i])
                dp[i] = dp[j] + arr[i];
        }
    }
    for (i = 0; i < N; i++)
        mx = max(mx,dp[i]);

    return mx;
}


TC : O(n^2), n: length(arr)
```

Input:
[1, 101, 2, 3, 100, 4, 5]

output: 106
(1 + 2 + 3 + 100)

MORE QUESTIONS